Dreams of Falling, Dreams of Love

The house where I learned about me...

Dreams of Falling,
Dreams of Love

Martin Petersilia

SeaStory Press

Printed in the United States of America

ISBN 978-1-936818-41-9

LCCN 2013946012

SeaStory Press

305 Whitehead St. #1

Key West. Florida 33040

www.seastorypress.com

To K.

Always...with no strings attached

Poems

WHEN WE WERE YOUNG

UNDER LINDENS

All the trees on the city block where I grew up
were linden trees.
Flowers filled the humid, early summer air with smells
of open jars of honey,
which drove the honeybees and hornets high above us
wild with wanting
for the most perfect nectar to the bee.

In brilliant afternoons, heat shimmered from sidewalks.
And fragrance oozed
from galaxies of tiny golden stars,
clustered, and suspended
in their universe of pale green leaves,
where the buzzing of bees increased, at last, to overmatch
the threatening whine of wasp wings.

When the last hot nights of May oozed into June,
the golden-honey smell oozed in, through open windows,
into front parlors,
and second-floor bedrooms without air-conditioning,
as the sounds of traffic moving along H Street died
together with the night voices
walking on feet down 5th Street, below our open bedroom windows.

The oozing-honey smell would cause our heads to spin,
until we could believe ourselves to be
in some deeper, cooler meadow where we were not.
Dreaming about apple trees hung low with bloom and fruit,
and white and purple clovers soft beneath our feet,
inhaling the perfume of linden trees on city streets,
we fell asleep.

FROM THE APPLE ORCHARD

When I was young
and there was country in Del Ray,
my grandmother had three apple trees.
My grandfather had planted them
when their house was built.

By the time that I was five or six,
they had all been planted thirty years.
By the time that I was five or six,
they were not sprayed
or pruned.

But, sprays and pruning hooks
were no longer needed,
because, as my grandmother said,
"Now, they 'just growed' …
like Topsy."

They were dearly loved,
but in their souls self-willed and stubborn,
and pretty much allowed
to go along in their own way,
as they and God saw fit.

At the end of every summer,
without complaint,
they gave, what seemed to me,
the most bountiful of harvests.
Their apples simply fell!

They had coddling moths,
the 'worm' within the apple.

Almost all were in some way
misshapen
with the apple blight.

Or such a thing
that neither we,
nor the apple trees,
ever did complain about
very much.

Most were reddish or striped after a fashion.
Some were yellow.
and some, unripe, were, really, … apple green.
They were small,
and I was small.

But to me they were God's apples,
and with them grandmother and I,
at the end of every summer,
made the most delicious apple sauce
that I have ever known.

Grandmother would cut out the "bad spots,"
core and peel them,
put them in a pot
with sugar and water "to cover"
and let them "slowly simmer, until soft."

My job was ever so much easier.
I only had to go around the yard and pick them up!
But don't you believe that old saying that
"Apples don't fall far from the tree."
Sometimes they would fall and roll, and roll, and roll.

They'd roll all the way out into the back alley
that ran behind the Rose of Sharon hedge.
I would pick them up in an old coal bucket,
watching the blackbirds in the open field which looked like it went on forever,
where my grandfather would soon build his new apartment house.

When we'd finished and the sauce was mushy and sweet,
grandmother would add her spices:
a little nutmeg, more cinnamon, and a dash of lemon juice, "to hold the color."
Then, sometimes, we would delight ourselves with hot apple sauce,
for breakfast in the morning.

Before I'd gotten big, our apple trees stopped growing.
Their branches snapped and broke as they grew old.
Their main trunks hollowed out and started to fall down.
And they were cut … first one, then two, then three,
and taken all away.

When I was young, and there still was country in Del Ray,
my grandmother had three apple trees.
They were dearly loved, but in their souls self-willed and stubborn.
They were pretty much allowed to go along
in their own way, as they and God saw fit.

They were old apple trees
that my grandmother said,
"Just growed, … like Topsy!"
And in the long, long years to come
so did I.

LEARNING THINGS

I was a brilliant child.
I hated school,
as much as I loved
being at my grandfather's house
for weeks on end
all the summer long.

Through all the days and nights
of sights and smells and sounds,
of mocking birds and whippoorwills,
of Bull Bay magnolias, and bumblebees in hollyhocks,
of new cut grass,
and roses.

I loved the sleeping porch,
where I would sit and swing,
and listen to cicadas chant their rhythms
as the rumbling wheels of boxcars rolled,
down the long slope of the tracks in Potomac sorting yard,
before they crashed, - coupling to a waiting train.

I loved shad roe,
and codfish cakes,
and fried eggs over easy,
consumed so eagerly,
together with the grownups' conversation
at the old tables in my grandmother's kitchen.

I loved the vegetables at dinner,
always overcooked in southern style,
ending in some mysterious culinary study
in shades of mostly brown.

(Sopping the pot-liquor with Sunbeam Bread,
until it was all gone.)

I loved the things that my grandfather taught me
in his garden.
They were things that I learned well.
He
was the first
of only two real teachers in my life.

But summer's sultry evenings on the swing
would always come to soon to end.
(I hated school.)
And in the first week of September,
every night , I cried myself to sleep,
"Please, Grandmother. I don't want to go."

LEARNING ME: AT UNIVERSITY

OUTSIDER

I am a child of the older age.
I am a man from the younger time.
I am the one called the solitaire drummer,
the magical mummer,
the mystery mime.
I am the outcast, inward bred,
the banner-bearer,
his tribes all fled,
a patriarch father, and yet,
unwed,
and a druid of deities long believed dead,
whose litanies still rhyme.

LONGING

My God came
Tall, dark and brooding.
Deity, bleeding kind,
Heals souls,
Rapes minds,
Eats hearts.

(But Love,
    as written on the page,
    could never be complete.)
Because there were
      no words   that you would hear.

Because
  there were
            no words to tell
How   beautiful!
  you   are.

And then,   for more than forty years,
  we
spoke
no words.

CLIMBING

When I'm looking down
from the room at the top,
then
ask me how much I will care,
that all of our climbing up
into high places
is *done*
on a winding stair.

SONG OR STORY

I woke up alone on Tuesday morning.
There was only
one can each of:
Campbell's Condensed Tomato soup
and
Iron City beer
left in the refrigerator.
(I wondered *why*
we were *refrigerating* soup.)

Beer bubbles over
when you heat it up.
But sitting at the breakfast table
and staring into space out our *one* back window,
I decided
Campbell's soup
had never
tasted quite this *good* before

Halfway through the *second* bowl,
I looked up , and saw:
the shapely foot, then, the ankle, calf and thigh
of
beautiful
black-haired, blue-eyed, long-legged, ... lovely
Cecelia Leahy,
stepping off the metal roof
and over the window sill
into the bath
just as the voice on the radio sang,
"She came in through the bathroom window ..."

Now,
That
was one *hell* of an opening line!
with,
or *without*
the soup!

But,   she
   had   not   come   for   me.

And after that,
nothing could quite live up to it again,
in song *or* story, …
either for Joe Cocker,
or for me.

Then it was Friday night again.
So Scott and I went drinking up in Georgetown,
at some bar
where they didn't serve Iron City,
and they didn't play
Joe Cocker
on the radio.

for Jon Damon

THE SECRET SHARER

Lying on our backs, in separate beds,
We kept our hands grasped tightly,
               in one another.
"I can feel your blood," you said.
"I'm afraid to let go," you said,
               (though I had thought the fear was all in me).
"Me, too," I said, and we held on
Palms pressed against each other,
The secret, sharing space,
               between
Together and alone.

SOTTO VOCE

If I only knew
Exactly what you wanted me to say,
There would be no need
To choose words,
Oh so carefully!
For there would be no need for words
At all.

SOME MORNINGS

I once had thought that I would always love you.
Yet,
I have cherished lovers long since
Then.
But on a sunny morning,
When I am stretching hard upon my bed,
I turn half-round
Anticipating
You.

THE COASTS OF AFRICA

FROM WASHINGTON, WITH A TICKET TO THE TAJ HOTEL

Got to get Away!
      (Maybe just one day)
From this honky town,
where life is ground —— down,
to someplace where the sun comes up,
      sun goes down
(red, maybe, —— gold maybe)
someplace where folks' skin
is a darker shade of —— brown,
someplace where a man can sit, —— down
under a coconut palm.
Africa maybe.
Lamu maybe.
Mombasa, maybe, —— maybe.
(Or maybe Dar es Salaam.)

MOMBASA: KILINDINI ROAD

A cock crows twice.
Morning smells arise,
of pastries frying deep in scented oils,
and coffee, teas, and cinnamon,
                    and spice.

With looming light,
the onyx sky has turned.
It fades through lilac, lavender to blue.
The Sun flames golden
                    on the silver Night.

From Zanzibar and Pemba, and Ceylon
the Ocean's roar rolls in.
The pied crow backs its wings
and brakes in flight, to settle softly
                    on a coconut frond.

Cats call. The holy muezzin cries. The silent night is gone.
The palm leaf bends,
then rises up again,
to fling its lacy fingers, at
                    the Dawn!

There is a church on Zanzibar. This church was built in the Old City, following the shortest war that history has recorded. The Sultanate surrendered in one minute and a half, agreeing with the British to end its trade in slaves. One half of the old slave market was purchased by a bishop. The second half was donated by a wealthy merchant who hoped, somehow, to save his soul. And so the church was built.

It was built in a neo-Gothic style, but constructed of coral-stone blocks, or "rag" as it is called, to adapt it to its place, lighted only by narrow windows that end in arabesques, — and, here and there above the altar, by the glow of oil lamps. Inside, the church seems dark and close, with air that smells of the sea, and old soil, and cloves and frankincense, and myrrh. The church altar was built around and above another stone, – an older place of meeting.

ON ZANZIBAR

In Zanzibar,
the old man stands, then kneels
and prays with folded hands
behind the altar stone.
Three quarters of a century of years, and more, are gone,
and he, alone,
remembers now.

He had a mother once.
(This I was told by another holy man,
who spends his life a priest
among the harbors of the coast.)
But she was sold,
there,
below the stone on which he prays.

With words that are deep mysteries to me,
on notes in melodies my soul recalls,
his people sing to God,
"Te Deum," and much more.
They sing their praise, and praise, and praise,
men on the right, children with their mothers on the left.
They sing, and they do not know.

22

They sing mysterious melodies in the gloom of the cathedral,
beneath the slender gothic lites
that end in arabesques.
They sing from note to note to note,
all un-arranged, but true.
And every angel voice is falling, falling
falling from its heaven to the earth.

They are singing, and they do not know.
I have been told, and I do know.
But he, alone, remembers, now as he lifts the sacred Host,
"In the old days of the Arabs, my mother,
here, was sold."
And the singing is too much, in melodies
that slowly crush your heart.

(July,1974)

IN LAMU

In the Bajun Archipelago
lies the ancient town of Lamu,
where the old fort is a prison
and the streets are dark at night.

I saw him once,
the lovely boy,
as the door to the house was opened,
the lamplight from within the room
reflecting in his eyes,

Reflecting
from the green silk robe
that fell down
from his shoulders
to his feet.

I saw him once,
the beautiful young man,
with hair that shone at midnight,
and skin
like powdered cloves,

His lips
deep red
and the black kohl of the harlots
smeared above the linings
of his eyes.

I saw him once,
in the Bajun town of Lamu.
I saw him in the lamplight,
once,
before the door was closed.

I wondered who he was.
I wondered
what he thought and felt
when the men who lied would come to him
and leave when they were done.

And I wondered who it might have been
who loved him
in his dreams,
in the old house by the prison,
where the streets are dark at night.

Or who he was
who loved him
in the sun.

A KIND OF WHITE BOY WHO COULDN'T EVER BE

BUTCH

"I love you, nigger!"
He said.
I looked down at the palms,
And then the backs,
Of my white hands.
(The "N" word,
Out of context.)
I saw the sadness
In his face,
And knew he did.

I THANK YOU, DR. SAMUEL WEEKS

It's one week workin'
and the blood still settles in small clots
within
my jaw. It's raw.
There is a palish yellow bruise, –
though not of easy notice, –
on my chin.
But, Heaven shall be praised!
That, after two excruciating days,
The Howard Dental School, –
or, –
more exact, –
the Clinic for Emergencies,
with ease
was able to extract
that tooth,
forsooth,
from out
my mout'.

CUZZINS

Llord Lorenzo Callendar and I used to play
The Game,
coming back from one of my theater shows,
or from one of his griot readings of African stories.

We would speak loudly
among our friends,
calling each other "Cuz," ——
until at last, *someone* would ask.

He, being rather stocky, and Jamaica dark,
Me, being pretty skinny, and pretty damn white,
we'd   …   hesitate,
then say together,

"We don't like
                to talk about it."
"We don't *like* to
                talk about it."
And when they'd left, and gone on home,
we would laugh, and laugh, and laugh!

Then he would look at me and say,
"You know, you *are* the kind of white boy
our parents always told us
couldn't ever be."

HYMN

Your song is sweet
as a spiritual to me,
when you pronounce my name.

The sound of your first breath
each time we meet anew,
swells
within the silence of my soul
and echoes,
in my renaissance in you.

I cradle you, oh love,
within my arms.
You rock me on the water.

(New Year's Day, 1977)

LEGACY

She screams at him
that he isn't,
"Any kinda' *real man !* "
still angry
that he let the white folks
sell her family away ...

centuries ago.

PLAYING FIELDS

The morning sun slants
against the brown earth of the playing fields.
In April, it is still cold in the mornings.
There is no one playing now.
Later in this day, with the warming sun,
the men will come.
White, beige, brown and black,
speaking Latin tongues,
speaking about soccer games,
speaking about their lack of jobs.
Not speaking English.
It is green and warm
in the south.
There was work in Nicaragua,
but the killing was too much.

(Washington, D.C. – Spring, 1986)

I can't remember what it was
that we were hollering about,
but I slammed the back room door
and left,
damning his black ass.

He caught me
on the top step of the stairs.
He slammed me up against the wall.
He put his hands around my throat,
and squeezed.

I was still yelling,
and choking,
and yelling,
and he was
damning me!

Nellie came running
out of her bedroom door,
hollering,
"What in the Name of Gaawd
is goin' on?!!"

Yelling for us to stop,
"Stop it! Stop it, Tony!
For God's sakes, Tony! Stop it!!!
You're gonna' kill him!!!"
And Tony stopped.

Tony stared into my eyes,
but kept his hands around my throat
and squeezed hard,
one more time.
And then, let go.

Nellie said, "For God's sakes, Tony!
Do you want to kill him ?!!"
I knew, then, that he didn't.
He would never hurt me now.
(He never did.)

And I would never go.

NORTH AND SOUTH FROM HERE

MORNING: FRENCHMAN BAY

Ten crows mob from out of a cloud.
Black, they cross the closed-in sky.
And disappear
as quickly as they came.

Morning mist hangs
as a pearl-soft curtain,
a theater's scrim, to hide the play
of life at the edge of the sea.

Grey air smells of ocean water.
Along the fog-bound coasts of Maine,
harbor seals bark
from unseen shelters.

Keeping guard from a high rock,
one seagull mews
above the sea-weeds
wave-strewn over the shingled beach.

AUTUMN ENDS IN MARYLAND

I watched my garden yesterday,
hushed in November,
soft and grey.
The last warm rain
before the winter's blast.

Damp carpets,
gold, and red, and brown,
settled snugly in
and down, –
among the mosses.

Slender leaves of grass
are Irish green
again,
for one brief season
under the cooling sun.

Only the azure aster
blooms bravely now.
The roses of October
are blown away
and gone.

Landlords worry constantly
about their property
which houses others,
about windows left ajar to vent stale air,
or the potted plants presenting summer's colors
from the railings of the front deck that wants to be a porch,
about too many flowers in the yard,
the flowers all the neighbors like so well,
and say the place never looked better,
and say how they walk by each day,
and how so many flowers
make them smile.

Landlords worry about,
"Who will take care of all those flowers
if you move?
Say, …
if you move.
If, say, you move in six,
or eight,
or, in ten years, you move?"
So,
landlords worry
because,
"There are just too many flowers."

Landlords worry
about why you replaced the leaking toilet,
and never asked,
and paid for it yourself;
about why you
replaced the leaking kitchen sink

and never asked,

and paid for it

when they had moved away three hundred miles;

and didn't ask,

either,

for any credit on your bill.

Landlords have to worry

about whether or not

you might have

too much furniture

and too many of your grandmother's old things

for an old place,

which are,

"a lot of pretty nice old things

and antiques and paintings,

and some pretty nice new ones, too."

But, maybe,

there are just too many.

And landlords worry about that window left ajar,

three inches,

over the tiled window sill

above the bathroom tub with the tiled surround,

the window you left ajar

to vent the stale and humid air that can cause black mold to build up

in an old place,

but which could let in

the Rains of Ranchipur

to stain the plywood floor under the once-upon-a-time beige carpet,

wall to wall,

that was already badly stained the day that you moved in.

But, after you have paid the rent on time
each month,
for more than seven years,
sometimes, when their houses are their social life,
landlords come to visit for an hour or two,
allowing as how there really are a lot of pretty flowers in the yard,
talking politics, because, after all,
the two of you do hold to the same politics
and friends can talk to one another in private about how
the Republicans really don't give a damn about the common man.
Though he's not quite sure how it is that you came to agree with him
on this.

Or why,
(since his eyes cannot see the color green)
last month,
when you didn't ask,
you painted the bathroom …

purple!

Landlords have to worry.

JUST IN TIME

My neighbor hurried past on Sunday morning.
"How are you?" she smiled.
"I'm fine," I said.
I was watering my plants. ("One is nearer God's heart in a garden … ")

"How are you?" I asked.
"I'm late for church …
                        as usual," she gasped.
"That's why I'm hurrying so!"

"God will wait," I said,
sounding like a sage.   (Believing it was true.)
And adding, after she had gone,
"The congregation won't,
                        but God will
                                    wait for you."

There had been proposals of marriage
once or twice,
perhaps a few times more,
from men she knew and liked.
But they had not seemed right to her
back then.
How was a marriage right
when the love was wrong?
When the idea of that love seemed wrong to her?
She had told them, "No,"
quietly,
and moved away.
To follow dreams
out into the wide, wide world.

She often returned to visit,
and here was her nephew, four,
sitting on the carpet
next to her chair, talking.
Oh! How she loved him!
The greatest joy ever brought to her heart.
He called her, "My sweet honey,"
and spent all his time with her
whenever she came home.
She knew things would change in his world,
and in him,
(too soon for her)
from that first day when he would go to school.

It was then she had decided
to leave the house
she had worked so hard

to bring to her idea of loveliness,
her *own* house.
She would move back home for *him*,
to be near him,
spending all the time she could,
with *him*,
in the next two years.

She would see him, always,
later in his life,
strong and tall and handsome,
with golden hair
(as she knew that he would be),
bringing home his bride
to introduce with pride to her
for her approval.
(And she *would* approve.)

Her mind was wandering,
thinking through her old ideas of love and loveliness.
She wondered if he would love her
quite like this,
if she had married all those years ago.
He was standing next to her now.
His breathing broke her reverie.
"Oh! My sweet honey!" her nephew said.
"You are so lovely!
I am so glad it's just the *two* of us,
and I don't have to share you at all,
with some old man!"

She looked down, and saw him,
smiling up at her.

She looked down, and saw him
looking up.
(He was smiling at her
through her tears.)

SNOW CROCUS IN VIRGINIA

There comes a day
near Valentine's,
when the air grows soft
and the wind blows,
fitfully, with unseasonable warmth from the south.

Star-pronged chalices lie un-lidded,
scattered in the grass, revealing gold,
filled,
as if by faerie fade, brim full
with one, first, draft of spring's intoxicating wines.

From cup to wide-flat open lilac cup,
quenching winter's long and deadly thirst,
reeking
of love, and the breath of honeys-yet-to-be,
bees drink.

STRINGS AND THE SOUTH WIND

for Cristina, – who plays a harp in Vera Cruz

CRISTINA'S HARP

Tonight the harps are played.
And tonight the harpers are playing.
Esta noche. In La Guaira,
and in Vera Cruz, and in Asunción. Y en mi corazón.

There was music
long ago when angels played in heaven.
And harpers played on Zion, and in the Peloponnese of the Greeks
and in Galicia of all the Spains, and through the halls of Tara, and in Donegal.

The soft air moves.
The song is drawn away.
The harpers drawn away,
the harps remain.

Tonight the songs come from the south.
Esta noche. And from the harps,
and heaven.
La música de los ángeles inunda mi corazón.

Tonight the harpers are playing,
and I am drawn away.
I go to where the earth is warm
and giving birth to palms.

I take it to my heart,
and my left arm aches. Y también mi corazón.
For the pain of joy and sorrow in the music,
the pain of life, or of loving too long. El inunda tu corazón!

And my eyes close.
And I am drawn away from now, from me, from heart.
Music becomes heart, my soul. Becomes my soul
as mourning became Electra.

When the harps are played
to joy over sadness,
to joy beyond sorrow,
tonight and tomorrow. O! Corazón!

If my heart stops,
tonight, the harp has broken it.
Tonight let no physician come to heart,
nor priest to seal my soul.

When I am placed along the ground
you will bring the harpers near,
and I will find the earth not cold,
but warm and soft and giving birth to palms.

And I will hear
the harp!
I will be drawn away
by the music of the angels. Oh! Corazón.

From La Guaira
by way of the Vera Cruz
into my own Asunción.
Cristina's harp! El arpa. La ofrezco a Dios! De mi corazón.

OLD COUNTRIES

THE EMIGRANT'S RETURN

I'm Irish long ago,
and there are times when whiskey
and the notes of Ireland's music
pull at my heart
and my resolve
that I will never cry.

At last,
with more than half
of my life's days gone by,
I wander home,
three lovely (mostly) Irish sisters
bringing me along.

Each day, I ride
at the back of the bus
(too many years growing older
with black folks in America),
drinking paper cups of
Paddy's Irish Whiskey, neat.

The music on the tape begins again:
old Irish songs, and new,
and later songs, written in times after
the Irish fled to the west,
when the music changed,
to songs of longing to return.

The sweet-sad songs
of the Irish in America:
"If you ever go across the sea to Ireland …
"I'll take you home again, Kathleen …
"I loved you as I never loved before …
when you were sweet, when you were sweet sixteen."

And I watch Ireland as she passes by,
a land of broken towers, broken dreams.
I dream a haunted land of ghosts, and saints and fairies.
Overwhelmed.
As I am overwhelmed in whiskey neat and sorrow,
and trying not to cry.

(A real man doesn't cry.)
For all life's lost connections,
(listening to the music on the tape)
thinking thoughts of my lost lovers,
thinking thoughts about my mother,
when *she* was sweet sixteen.

(Killarney – October, 2005 / near Tralee – April, 2012)

Carol Anne walked in and out,

in and out,

stopping,

gazing up at the tower, floodlit,

turning,

walking in and out

of the small, stone-floored lobby

of the Albergo Ariston on Cardinal Maffi Street.

She felt, she said,

as if she were standing in a movie set

in Hollywood.

But this was not a movie set.

"I've died and ended up here," she thought.

She *could* have died, she thought,

on the long, hot train ride north.

Eleven hours on the planes, changing at Madrid,

the local train to Roma Termini,

he forgetting, until the very last minute,

to validate the Euro-rail pass,

running the half-mile length of the platform, yelling over his shoulder

for her to jam her valise into the train doors

to stop its departing,

which she had done, until he ran the half-mile back, panting,

pulled their luggage on board, and the train left,

crowded at rush hour,

crowded for four hours more,

even in first class, hot and crowded,

along the dusty coasts of Lazio and Tuscany from Rome.

And waiting another hour,

standing, waiting,

at the station,

for the *only* taxi running

on the eve of San Ranieri's feast.

(He'd kept it a surprise that they would arrive on the holy day.)

She was much better,

after their ten o'clock dinner, al fresco,

at the trattoria down the street,

where her food had been served

by the *handsomest* young waiter,

who was working his way through the University.

Yes! She felt she could easily have died on the train coming up from Rome.

But she was here now.

(He had asked her where it was in Italy she would most like to go.)

And it was *not* a set in Hollywood,

or,

thank God, in Las Vegas!

The web-site they had found on Pat's computer had not lied …

"In the shadow of …"

She was standing in the floodlit shadow now,

or would have been

except the tower,

which *was* leaning,

was leaning

away from her.

She could walk around to the other side.

The night was warm.

It was the eve of San Ranieri's feast.

Soon,

looking up she saw,

above the tower,

to the south and out over the river

fireworks were exploding

into the midnight sky.

Behind the ticket counter in the stazzione,
the young woman with blond hair smiled,
saying its would be quicker and less trouble
to take the train to Pontedera
and board the local bus from there.

If they followed the tourist guidebooks,
they would have to take two trains,
wait for the connecting service, and *still* take a local bus.
She was a stunner!
He agreed, wanting to believe that she was right.

And she *had* been right!
His sisters had just located seats among the morning commuters travelling on to
Firenze
and *he* had barely lifted the bags to the rack above their heads,
when the train pulled into Pontedera
and it was time to haul them down again.

He rushed across the street to buy their tickets,
before the bus arrived,
wondering again why women
would bring along so *many* clothes
for a trip of only fourteen days.

Carol Anne and Edith were looking out the window
at the undulating hills,
with grain-fields golden at the end of June,
stretching out past their dividing lines of cypress trees,
out to the horizon.

They sat, looking out,
as with each turn
of the narrow, winding road,
the bus gained altitude
against the mountain toward the south.

Carol Anne turned to look at *him*.
"It is *everything* I *hoped* that Tuscany would be," she said.
He sighed.
He was glad.
He hadn't disappointed them.

They really thought that the trip was wonderful!
And it *was* wonderful,
as the driver shifted to a lower gear,
and the bus climbed in circles,
each circuit higher up the mountain.

They would not be disappointed here,
in the ancient city, — old as the Etruscans, — waiting for them at the top.
He sighed again.
They would not be disappointed here.
So *many* beautiful things to see.

The bus stopped in the open piazza,
from which they could look down the side of the mountain
and out across the countryside
for miles and countless miles,
as the Etruscans had once done.

They would not be disappointed *here*.
They were on Volterra!

The Cove of Cork, which lies just inside the Atlantic Ocean shore on the southwest coast of Ireland, is, along with San Francisco Bay in California and Botany Bay in New South Wales, one of the greatest natural harbors in the world. There was a time when all the naval ships of all the navies of the British Empire could have anchored comfortably in her waters, side by side. In the Eighteenth Century, the Cove was, in fact, a major base for the British Navy, against the rebellion of Ireland, or invasion by the armies of the Spanish or the French. In the Nineteenth and early Twentieth Centuries, the little seaport city of Cove became the last European port of call for ships that were sailing to Halifax and Quebec, and Boston and beyond. Renamed "Queenstown" to honor Queen Victoria after her arrival there in 1849, on her first visit to Ireland, the city's name reverted to the Irish spelling of "Cobh" in 1922 when the Irish Free State became the nation's unwilling reality.

Though scarcely twenty thousand ever called her their home, in the course of one hundred years, nearly two and a half million persons walked through her cobbled streets and down to her piers to board a sailing ship or, later, a steamer of the Cunard or the White Star Lines, leaving out of Ireland for a chance at a new life in America or one of the Dominions. Two and one half million people, each of them with a story.

In 1892, Annie Moore and her two younger brothers left from the pier at Queenstown, and became the first registered persons from any nation to enter the United States through New York's immense new immigration station on Ellis Island.

Within the space of barely three years, in April of 1912, and again, in May of 1915, the city of Cobh bore direct witness to events that we have come to know as the two greatest maritime disasters of the Twentieth Century, including witness to the anchoring of the ship with the most famous name of all the ships of history.

COVE HARBOR

My mother's uncle missed the boat
at Cobh,
in the old days,
when Cobh was Queenstown,
when "First Class" paid its own way
and had a different meaning,
but steerage tickets paid for everything else,
and kept the liners sailing,
and the emigrants sailing to their dreams
of what life would become for them in America.

My mother's uncle missed the boat at Cobh,
standing on the pier,
waving his ticket above his head
at the crew of the last tender,
and they,
refusing to turn round
for his being late,
or all the rest of them
would miss their boat to America,
the Royal Mail Steamer that gleamed in the late morning light,
standing,
steam up.
in the roads,
waiting for the last steerage tender,
waiting, with greater regard,
for her last mail.

She anchored for one hundred-twenty minutes.
More, and she would not make the record.
It would take too long to bring her in
and turn her around at the deepwater pier,
where he waved his ticket over his head,
but they would not turn around
for him.
"Sweet Jesus!" he said.
"I've missed me boat!"
And "Jesus," they said on the tender.
"It's too bad for him,
but he's missed the boat this time!"

My mother's uncle watched
as the tender pulled away
toward the great ship
that lay at anchor,
waiting,
steam up, in the roads,
for her last tender,
full of Irish emigrants
waving their good-byes to Cobh,
waving in sorrow at the town of Cobh,
with its cathedral to Saint Colman at the top
and the pubs behind,
waving in sorrow,
at him.
"Too bad! He's missed the boat. This time.
But the Lord knows what He is doing," they said.
"God has reasons," they said.
"And whose fault is it but his own?
He's the one who was late."

And, "Sweet Jesus!" he said to himself.
He'd have to sail the next time
on his ship of dreams.
He'd sail on her the next time.
But she,
The Great Ship,
sailed only once from Cobh.

They sang about her,

later,

in the mountains of Virginia

and in the mountain coves of Tennessee.

They sang for unknown souls,

and for the poverty that they knew as surely as their own.

They raised their voices singing:

"Put the poor below.

They's the first that had to go.

Oh, wasn't it sad!

When the great boat went down."

(begun at Cobh, 11:30 AM, April 11th, 2012)

WEDDING RING

Wed me with the Ring of Kerry!
And I will cleave to Ireland all my life.
Not expecting
ever to be richer,
except in spirit,
or to know a greater health,
except in my heart of hearts
with Ireland as my love.

But I will plight my troth,
comprehending,
as her dowry given:
on her heathered hillside,
near to the silver-mirrored lake,
through the gap in her gold-gorsed mountains
where the mists of morning reek high above,
and down to the sounding sea,
all the lovely, little roads of Ireland
will,
while I am true,
belong to me.

Oh! Wed me with the Ring of Kerry,
that long, wild road that leads me home round Iveragh,
to have,
in mind,
and hold
within my soul.
And Ireland to love,
and cherish, unto death.

MEAD

Speak with me awhile
of love.
And share with me a parting glass
of the honeymoon wine,
and a second glass after,
And your body after,
lying next to mine, lying in mine,
after,
and your soul
next to mine,
and your soul in mine,
after,
and mine in yours,
after.
Ever after.

DEPARTURES AND REUNIONS

For John Bacon

RENEGADE

You were the last to go,
and I was arguing with you
to stay.
(I wanted you to stay.)
You sat on your motorcycle,
looking like a renegade.

You were the last to go.
All God's wonderful lost boys
were leaving now.
I would,
one more time,
be left alone.

The chapter house was gone.
The thing could not
be saved,
its time all
past.
You had your life ahead.

And I had mine
to live,
"beyond the pale"
through all the decades
in between,
before we spoke again.

The voice on the telephone
was yours,
a voice from the beginnings of my life.
"We're going to have a party.
It's my job to tell you,
and see to it you come."

So I came to the party,
not knowing why.
But,
you
had asked.
And I could not say, "No."

Through all your life,
you had grown, a man,
with a man's responsibilities,
those things from which,
in fear,
I had always fled, and run away.

You said,
"I've worried over you
 through all my life.
The last time that we met
we had a fight."
Then, I remembered, too.

But you have been a man,
and, after all those years,
I , still, am only a lost boy.
And, – just to me,
you are, still,
a renegade.

LETTERS

In my mind
I think I know
that I will not receive
a letter back
from you.

But, my heart
won't let it be.
My heart can't
let you
go.

On Sunday mornings,
watering the flowers
that bloom in my front yard,
I stop
to lift the mail-box lid.

Believing,
like Pandora,
that I might find
Hope,
still trapped inside.

I HEARD HIS VOICE

I called him,
fifty years almost
to the day
when we first met,
to say
that knowing him
had set the course
of every thing
that I had ever done.

Each day,
within my mind,
I tried to practice
what I'd say.

I had written him
to tell him
I had loved him all my life.
I wrote a second time, to tell him many things,
a catalogue of what that life had been.
No answer came.
I wrote again.
No answer still.

So, at last,
I knew.

I called him
on the telephone.

And when I asked for him,
a soft, small boy's voice answered,

tentative and shy.
"Yes? " he said.
"Is it you?" I asked.
"Yes," he said again.
"It's me," I said.
And then the small voice changed,
to the wonderful full voice
that I had always known,
the voice filled with
a strong young man's bravado,
the voice that had
protected him
from all the pain of life.

"Aw, come on, man,
I don't want to talk to you," he said.
"I don't want you to
keep sending me all this stuff," he said.
"I'm too old for this shit,"
he said.
And he was gone.

And he was gone.
And all that I could hear inside my mind
was a small boy's voice
that answered "Yes ?"
and another voice,
that voice I loved so well,
that said,
"I am too old ..."

OH! CALIFORNIA!

I have no idea,
really,
why
I am going
there.

I am
too old
to begin my life again,
and almost without courage
or desire enough to try.

I am travelling to
our New World's grand illusion
of Ireland's Isles of Youth
recaptured
out in the Golden West.

I travel to a place where palm trees bloom
and long lost dreams
are found,
and dreamed again,
on celluloid.

He lives there now;
that is enough.
And I am going,
going west along.
Oh! California!

God stretches out
His great,
creating hand.
He places it
great palm down,
beyond the ridgeline of the mountains,

                    sun

              the

       up

pulling

to re-create His dawn
above their eastern slope.

Then, in His charity reverses His great hand,
palm up,
to push the under-ceiling of the sky,
and prove again
the wonder
of His wide and holy place

that is

in all the spaces in between.

In the cars along the daytime length
of the Coast Starlight (express)
passengers sleep,
and talk (too loud),
as if everyone needed to know
the family business
(all of it).
And they are riding,
and reading on their laptops,
and on their cell-phones,
and in their paperbacks.
They are
plugged in,
staring straight ahead,
and no one is seeing California.
The train pulls out from Santa Clara,
across and up
into the Pajaro Valley,
where the raspberry and blackberry vines grow
under arches of plastic wrap
and the strawberry fields go on (forever),
and the Mexican field laborers go on
forever, (bent)
picking strawberries.
The slightly past middle-aged woman with the fading red hair
from a bottle,
goes on chattering forever (too loud),
as if her cell phone were a tin can
at one end of a cotton string,
and I am praying (silently)
that her battery will go dead, before her father passes on,
and we have to hear about his funeral, too,

and not just the purchasing of the burial plot.
And the rest are just still
typing on their laptops,
and thumbing texts on their cell-phones, too,
and it is as the Albanian concierge in the small hotel in Florence said
one night at 2AM.
"They will all go home, but they will go home
without memories."
Except for one small Asian boy,
who is seven years old,
who talks incessantly,
gloriously,
about trains.
He is watching California.
And he is watching
everything.
When he grows old,
he will remember
childhood trains.
And he
will have
memories.

DOWN: THE 9TH OF NOVEMBER

The train drops down from the mountains' crest.
The Santa Lucias are bare mountains,
with oaks growing along the creek beds,
down their sides
and at their bases.
The train descends in great S-curves.
Everyone is looking now,
looking, — at California.

Everyone is quiet now, and watching, —
except the children,
who talk to one another
about the cattle and the sheep,
and count the tunnels (five of them),
one by one,
as the train passes through.
It eases down
to the Great Southern Pacific Horseshoe Curve
at San Luis Obispo.

The California men's prison
lies down, at the edge of the track,
surrounded by walls
of razor wire, and watchman's towers.
The children talk to one another.
"Prisons are so *cool!*" says the oldest girl,
who is nine, and has blond hair.
(Her mother looks surprised.)
"I don't suppose she's ever been to one," I say as our eyes meet.
She shakes her head,
and looks away.

There is a farm with guinea fowl,
and Cal Poly State University, on both sides of the track,
with tennis courts,
and cross country runners (in shorts in November),
and more cattle, and goats,
and a horse corral.
The children have stopped talking.

And the sun slides down
to a lower angle,
toward its perihelion.
The sky is clouding over from the west.
Soon, it's difficult to see
what is growing in the shadowy rows.
But on the service roads are rows
of pickup trucks
and, near by, Mexicans.
The valleys of California are fertile.
And everywhere,
they are growing Mexicans.

I visited the Getty yesterday,
and watched the statues of the Greeks

                (at the Roman villa).

They say good things come,

                in small packages.

But I'm wondering

                how

there ever

                were

any more Greeks.
I mean,
with their things

                so small and all.

I mean,
maybe   (they're mostly all *Roman* copies),
the Romans really

                were

scared of the Greeks,
or were mad

                and just getting back

at the Greeks
for being
smarter and better looking,
and better

                sculptors.

But God!
If:
you

had shoulders
         and a butt and
thighs
         that
looked like

                              That!
Who'd give a damn about: aqueducts
                             and roads to Parthia
                             and arches
(except the arch of your back.)

And I'd say, "Baby!
we'll just have to work
with what you've got!
We'll just have to
adopt
         a kid."

And raise him as if
he really were
a Greek …

Smarter and better looking, than
the Romans
in America.

I read Ferlinghetti Friday afternoon,
and again,
on Sunday
late at night.
(I bought the book for Dick,
at City Lights.
before I took the train down south
from San Jose.)
And, well,
it seems as if Ferlinghetti
has already said it all.
And I'm wondering why
I never
read
Ferlinghetti at twenty
when Dick tried to get me to
read him,
but didn't tell me
who
wrote the poem.
So now I've read him.
(And he's read me.)
And I guess I'd better just stop writing now.
(There's no need to make a bigger fool of myself.)
Because
Ferlinghetti's already said it
all about life
in America.
Even if he didn't exactly
understand
                how
                        to put it

                down
on   the page.

DREAMS OF FALLING

I lie with my chest pressed
flat against the ground
at the edge of
The Cliffs of Moher,
at the verge
above the wild Atlantic roar
and think for one wild moment
that I might
hurl
      myself

       beyond,
to stoop like the peregrine in ecstasy,
down,
down

down to the foam
of the dark-waved sea,

before I spread my unseen angel wings
and fly!

Yes,
I have flown before

in falling dreams,

the dreams I used to dream
when I was three and four,

wherein:

I climbed up
winding stairs of foot-worn, rain-washed stone
to the height of the highest battlement
of the highest curtain wall
of a nameless grey-stoned (Irish) castle
that towered far above the grass-greened swale.

And I pulled myself over the parapet
of the nameless
grey-stoned
(Irish)
castle,
and threw myself out
and into the misty air,
arms spread and falling
down,
down,

down

until I flew!

Or,
in those chance day-nights
when gravity
and downdrafts
overmatched
the uplift of the thermals against my unseen wings,
I jolted
wide awake,
just as I crashed spread-eagled
into the soft-green (Irish) sod.

II: LIONS IN VOLTERRA

When I was four,
I had never been
to Venice, or Volterra,
except, perhaps, in other lives
except, perhaps, in dreams I dreamed for years.
But it must have been
Volterra,
for there was no water there.
Only narrow, sun-baked lanes
and ancient walls
of tawny, sun-baked stones.
There were
 no banners of St. Mark.

+

But   there   were

                                                                        Lions.

+

Fiercely snarling tawny lions
with great manes, running.
Running
over sun-baked stones
(As I was running)
through narrow,
twisting, sun-baked lanes
that slowly filled
with people running   slowly,
screaming,
slowly,
and pursued by   lions.

(As I ran,   alone)
except for one
great-maned and tawny,
fiercely snarling lion.

He ran,

pursuing me,
closing the distance

until I fell (again)
over the same, small, out-pulled chair
(over which I always fell)
by the (same-small)
wooden table
in the (same-small)
street café
at the top of the three-step stair.
And, as the great lion mouth
with white teeth shining
(like great white knives, shining)
closed in
over mine,
(five years old now)
I jolted
(sweating)
                    Wide awake!

We moved from the house on 5th Street
when great-grandmother died,
from the house with the old victrola
where we played songs by Victor Herbert
and danced in the hall by the stairs.
We had no television then
or National Geographics
until after
we moved to Virginia,
where I don't remember
having dreams at all.
I do not know why the dreams stopped.
And I do not know
how it could come to pass
that,
once upon a time,
I could fly
from castle walls in Connaught,
or run from lions
under the Tuscan sun.

DREAMS OF LOVE

PILLOW FIGHT

I had a dream last night.
You and I lay together
in a big brass bed,
in a room with many windows
that looked out on the sea.

We had a pillow fight,
and wrestled as we laughed.
You touched me then,
and I made love to you.
Then *we* made love.

It is
the only dream I've had
where we
made love.
It is the only dream

I've ever had
where
anyone
made love
to me.

SEAN IN OLYMPUS

If I were Zeus,
I would lift you up like Ganymede
into my heaven,
to the wine and music of the Gods,
to jealousy
and hot debate,
and,
always,
love and passionate embrace.
But
not ever,
pain.

I will sail to Ephesus, and write a Book,
My Love,
in my old ages,
old beyond belief to those who knew me
when I was the youngest one,
and to those who look upon me now.

Here, in this island,
there are many eyes,
but none
so ancient as my own,
nor one-half old enough to remember us
the way we were,
or to have gazed upon Your face,
within whose lifting up
all worlds began.

And I will write a Book
of You,
My Love,
as I remember yet
each word You spoke.
And I will write them
in the story that I tell,
for every word You spoke to me
was,
"Love."

From that first afternoon,
when You turned to look at me, and asked,
"What do you want?"
our lives went on,

leading always to that other day,
when, through our tears,
You gave us,
as You loved us best,
to one another
in the midst of the howling storm,
while the earth shook.

And the word You screamed was,
"Why?"
and the word I heard
was, "Forsaken."
But *I* was there!
As I was
always
there,
at Your feet,
or with my head leaning
on Your shoulder.

You left us then.
But I believed,
and You came back to me,
changed,
while I remained as I had ever been.
Was I as You wanted me to be?
(Had You wanted me to hear?)
You said,
" … What if that man should remain
                    the same …?"

And when You left us for the second time,
I took Your mother with me,
into Asia.

For love of You,
I stayed with her,
through all her silent years,
until she could not bear the separation longer,
and, for love of You,
she followed You away,
and far away from tears,
while I remain
speaking with the Greeks in their own tongue,
(as I have learned to do)
until
You come for me.

And I will write this Book for You,
My Love,
for I can still remember
every word
You spoke to them
as I remember
every word
You spoke to me.
Your every word was love.
Love of Your words
is all I have become,
and all I am,
encompassing my all.

Your word has saved me
from the sword.
"Love."
Your word has saved me

from the flaming oil at the Latin Gate.
"Love!"
Your word has saved me from myself.
"Oh, Love!"

Now I begin to write
this Book of You, for You,
 My Love,
the song I've longed to sing to You myself.
For it must be that I have always loved You.
And it must be
I am beloved still!
(How I miss Your hand upon my arm!)

Oh! Kyrie!
Forget me not! Your lover
                          left behind.

+   +   +

"In the beginning was the Word.
And the Word was with God.

And the Word was God … "

                          (And all Your words were,   "Love!")

for K.

LOVE BEYOND DESIRE

My God came
tall, dark and brooding.
Deity, bleeding kind,
heals souls,
rapes minds,
eats hearts.

He is tall and dark.
His eyes
murmur magic
and the mystery of ages.
His look compels me to obedience,
and love beyond desire.

His beauty eats my heart.
It hurts to watch
such beauty
that my soul, and mind, and body,
ache to touch.
And I am terrified to look away.

He smiles.
He knows
how little of life, and death,
and love,
I know.
He knows what I fear.

He laughs at my pretended innocence.
He calls me, "hypocrite" – in the kindest way.
He tries to teach.
I cannot learn,
for I am drowning in his eyes
and the smell of his shoulders.

He is tall
and dark
and handsome.
He is Hades,
the final God,
who calls all things unto himself, at last.

I will die if he does not take me
with him,
to the darkest caverns of his soul,
where he will hold me hard within his arms,
and show his love to me,
and give me peace.

(Washington D.C. – May, 1962 / Arlington, Virginia – May, 2011)

MARTIN PETERSILIA lives in Arlington County, Virginia, where he works and gardens in the 440 square feet of "Late Bloomers Cottage," which he rents and which some of his neighbors believe washed up on a high tide from Key West — of which he also dreams.

photo: Mary Swift

ACKNOWLEDGEMENTS

My beautiful, brave, intelligent, enduring sisters: Patricia Petersilia, Carol Spencer and Edith Mayo, who really are best friends, who have always looked after me far more than I could ever deserve.

My lifetime friend, Snow Philip (like the USN missile frigate), who through the years has listened, loved and given the best advice, whether I took it or not, and who also likes me because I know how to spell her last name. Joy Ford Austin, ΠΚΑ brother Hank Bosma, Mark Jackson, Nicole Stevens, Simone Lasswell and Elena Tscherny for a lifetime of encouragement, affection, concern and "Just putting up with me."

ΠΚΑ brother, Ray Lupo, whose chance remark hit me like a mule kick, and started my putting this book down on paper.

Natasha Atkins, who said "Oh here! Just take my old laptop!", so I could make changes and stop copying everything over in longhand.

Heather Spence for staffing and arranging the enclosed song sheet of "Out of My Blues." Editor/publisher Sheri Lohr, of SeaStory Press, whose expertise was essential to getting through the process.

Pisa, Galway, Mombasa and Zanzibar for inspiration.

ΠΚΑ brother, John Bacon and his wife Carolyn, who have listened to all of these poems, read them all, talked with me about them all and kept them ALL in a 3-ring binder. And who keep asking, "When the hell does the book come out?" (Thanks guys!)

Sean, who talked to me for 3 hours last night at the bar.

Tony, who never stopped loving me.

K., to whom I owe the fact that I am still here, to whom this book is dedicated and who is still the hero of all my life.